The Trial of the Catonsville Nine

A PLAY

By Daniel Berrigan

Text prepared for the production
By Saul Levitt

SAMUEL FRENCH, INC.
25 WEST 45TH STREET   NEW YORK 10036
7623 SUNSET BOULEVARD HOLLYWOOD 90046
LONDON   TORONTO

THE TRIAL OF THE CATONSVILLE NINE, by Daniel Berrigan, opened at Good Shepherd-Faith Church, New York, on January 31, 1971, and at the Lyceum Theatre, New York, on June 2, 1971. The Phoenix Theatre, T. Edward Hambleton, Managing Director, and Leland Hayward produced the play, which was directed by Gordon Davidson, with scenery by Peter Wexler, costumes by Albert Wolsky, lighting by Tharon Musser. Text for the New York production was prepared by Saul Levitt and the production stage manager was Daniel Freudenberger. The cast was as follows:

DANIEL BERRIGAN .... *Ed Flanders*

PHILIP BERRIGAN .... *Michael Kane*

DAVID DARST .... *Leon Russom*

JOHN HOGAN .... *Barton Heyman*

THOMAS LEWIS .... *Sam Waterston*

MARJORIE MELVILLE .... *Gwen Arner*

THOMAS MELVILLE .... *Joe Ponazecki*

GEORGE MISCHE .... *Richard Jordan*

MARY MOYLAN .... *Nancy Malone*

DEFENSE .... *David Spielberg*

JUDGE .... *William Schallert*

WITNESS .... *Mary Jackson*

PROSECUTION .... *Davis Roberts*

MARSHALS .... { *Peter Gorwin* *James O'Connell* *Harry Spillman* }

The play was originally created in the experimental New Theatre For Now program produced by Center Theatre Group at the Mark Taper Forum, Los Angeles, in August, 1970.

3

CHARACTER DESCRIPTIONS

DANIEL BERRIGAN: 49, Jesuit priest and poet—aware of his personal magnetism—gaunt and ascetic with an impish sense of humor

PHILIP BERRIGAN: 47, Josephite priest—tall, massive, handsome, an impatient and fearless man with a radiant and irresistible good nature

DAVID DARST: 26, brilliant Harvard scholar—taught as a Christian Brother—ingenuous, clean-cut

JOHN HOGAN: 33, former Maryknoll brother—the quietest and most retiring of the Nine—gentle man trained as a carpenter

THOMAS LEWIS: 28, genial and boyish—former star halfback trained as an artist—taught subject in inner city schools and Catholic colleges

MARJORIE MELVILLE: 38, looks much younger, former Maryknoll nun—short and dainty, she radiates wholesome charm with an underlying shrewdness

THOMAS MELVILLE: 37, former Maryknoll priest—husband of Marjorie—strong, direct, giving an impression of solid respectability

GEORGE MISCHE: 32, massive, cocky, flamboyant—had worked with delinquent youths, widely traveled—most bellicose of the Nine

MARY MOYLAN: 32, graduated from Johns Hopkins as a nurse—impeccably groomed and the image of middle-class American wholesomeness

DEFENSE: pragmatic, intense, flamboyant, deeply committed to his clients, with a history in the civil rights movement

JUDGE: mid-sixties, eager to be liked by everybody—fatherly and painfully courteous

PROSECUTION: concise, dignified, careful to preserve his firm reasonableness

WITNESS: matronly clerk—dedicated civil servant

MARSHALS: court attendants

4

The Trial of
the Catonsville Nine

AT RISE: DANIEL BERRIGAN *stands at pulpit-like reading
desk with the other eight* DEFENDANTS *silhouetted
behind him.*

DANIEL BERRIGAN. On a June morning, I lay before
the altar in the chapel—to be ordained a priest—and the
voice of Cardinal Cushing shook the house like a great
war horse. His hands lay on my head like a stone. I remember a kind of desolation, the cold of the floor on
which I stretched like a corpse, while the invocation of
the saints went over me like a tide, a death. Would
these bones live? I arose to my feet and went out into
the sunshine and gave my blessing to those who had
borne with me, who had waited for me. A most unfinished
man. What would it mean to be a Catholic? Who would
be my teacher? It was, finally, the world, the world we
breathe in, the only stage of redemption, the men and
women who toil in it, sin in it, suffer and die in it. Apart
from them, as I came to know, the priesthood was a
pallid, vacuumatic enclosure, a sheepfold for sheep. (*Dis-
cards the reading desk.*) Priests? Why priests kept their
peace, muttered the Mass, sidestepped queasily the public
horror, made Jesus mild as milk, a temple eunuch. I don't
want to miss the action, but I must tell you my brother
Phil and I were in jail at the same time last year—he
for that little business of pouring blood on draft records

NOTE: This is a play about real people, all of whom (except David Darst) are still alive. In the New York
production some attention was paid to the physical
resemblances as described on page 4, but what is more
important is the essence and spirit of the characters
and not physical likenesses.

and I for marching on the Pentagon. Those prison blue jeans and denim shirts! It's a clerical attire I highly recommend for a new church. As Camus said— (*Laughs.*) I love to talk to people but I've got to get to a burning. *Oremus pro fratribus in periculo.* (DEFENDANTS *begin in pantomiming the burning of draft files;* DANIEL BERRIGAN *crosses* L.) Imagine nine felonious Catholics, jerky, harried as Keystone Cops, running out of a building bearing baskets heaped with trash, dumping them out, setting them alight, dancing like dervishes around the fire. The TV cameras ground it out, those four or five minutes when our past went up in flames whirling like ashes down a parking lot, then sober. As the flames died we joined hands praying, "Our Father who art in heaven." The film impounded rests in peace in FBI archives.

(MARSHALS *enter with American flag and witness rails.* PROSECUTION *and* DEFENSE *enter and cross to desks.* EACH DEFENDANT *moves* D. *as his name is called.*)

TAPE. Criminal Action No. 28111, the United States of America against Daniel Berrigan. . . . How do you plead?
DANIEL BERRIGAN. Not guilty.
TAPE. Philip Berrigan?
PHILIP BERRIGAN. Not guilty.
TAPE. David Darst?
DAVID DARST. Not guilty.

(JUDGE *enters and crosses to box.*)

TAPE. John Hogan?
JOHN HOGAN. Not guilty.
TAPE. Thomas Lewis?
THOMAS LEWIS. Not guilty.
TAPE. Marjorie Melville?
MARJORIE MELVILLIE. Not guilty.
TAPE. Thomas Melville?
THOMAS MELVILLE. Not guilty.
TAPE. George Mische?

GEORGE MISCHE. Not guilty.

TAPE. Mary Moylan?

MARY MOYLAN. Not guilty.

(*Gavel.* DEFENDANTS *greet one another and sit* U. R.
JURY *cross onto stage. LIGHTS indicate realistic
courtroom.*)

JUDGE. The court will come to order. The jury panel
will take their places.

DEFENSE. (*Crosses up onto stage.*) With regard to jury
selection, Your Honor, we wish to make one brief statement. The defendants will not participate in any way in
the selection of the jury. That will be a matter between
the court and the U. S. attorney.

JUDGE. You do not wish to have the benefit of striking
out names you object to?

DEFENSE. We are abstaining completely from the jury
selection.

JUDGE. Very well. This jury will now be seated. (JURY
enters the jury box; DEFENSE *crosses back to desk.*)
Members of this jury, the United States Government has
commenced a prosecution against nine defendants. The
indictment charges in three counts the following offenses:
that the defendants did willfully injure and commit dep-
redation against property of the United States; and willfully and unlawfully obliterate records of the Selective
Service System, Local Board No. 33, located in Catonsville, Maryland; and did willfully and knowingly inter-
fere with the administration of the Military Selective Service Act of 1967, by removing and burning the records
of Local Board No. 33 located in Catonsville, Maryland,
and by disrupting the official activities at the location of
the Local Board No. 33. The indictment further charges
that the defendants aided and abetted one another in
committing these alleged offenses. (MARSHALS *bring in
trash burners and boxes of charred ash—the evidence.*)
Each of the defendants has pleaded not guilty to these
charges. Accordingly, the burden of proof is upon the

government to prove the guilt of any of the defendants beyond a reasonable doubt.

(WITNESS *crosses to* C. *witness rail.* MARSHAL *swears* WITNESS *on Bible.*)

DANIEL BERRIGAN. (*Standing in front of* U. L. *bench.*) There's the evidence—those boxes of paper ash, the size of infant caskets I've seen. . . . Our trial was a question of facts, as such serious matters should be.

WITNESS. We had just come back from lunch. A gentleman came up the steps. I looked at him, and I said: "Could I help you, sir?" Before I could say anything else, all of these people came in. I asked them not to come in. I begged them not to come in the office, but they did. I was so confused and upset at that point. They utterly terrified us. We were just terrified. Of course, they immediately went to the files. I noticed one gentleman was carrying a trash burner. I begged them not to take the files. I begged them. One of them went right over to the files, and I could see him read the label on the 1-A Qualified drawer. He just emptied all those sheets right into the trash burner.

PROSECUTION. Please explain to the jury what a 1-A is.

WITNESS. Well, a person is 1-A when he really is not eligible for any other classification. Really there is nothing else we can find to put him in, frankly. I begged them and pleaded with them, but it was to no avail, and I might say that I have never been treated with such bad manners in my whole life, and with such disrespect or uncharity.

JUDGE. Strike it out. The defendants are not being tried for their manners.

PROSECUTION. What happened after they emptied the drawers?

WITNESS. I took hold of the trash burner, and I tried to pull it away, but I could not get it away from them, naturally. And in the scuffle I cut my leg and my hand. Then they ran down the stairs. I followed to the edge of the building and saw the fire, and I came running back up, and I said to the girl: "My God, they are burning our records."

PROSECUTION. And the 378 files taken would include all information necessary to draft young men?

WITNESS. That is right; everything that concerns a man.

PROSECUTION. What effect on the functioning of Local Board No. 33 has the incident of May 17 had?

WITNESS. It has given us a tremendous amount of work, and it certainly has inconvenienced our boys.

PROSECUTION. Have you yourself done any work in restoring those files?

WITNESS. I would estimate that in the general reconstruction, getting the papers from the Armed Forces, making lists, reconstructing the cover sheets, writing them all up again—all of this—I would estimate that, myself, alone, I have spent at least eighty hours. The other clerks spent about forty hours working with me. We also had three supervisors from State Headquarters working for three weeks.

PROSECUTION. Have you finished reconstructing these 378 files, as of today?

WITNESS. No, sir.

DEFENSE. (*Crosses up onto stage.*) Mrs. Boyle, at the time of the action about which you testified, what did the several people who came into the office say to you?

WITNESS. There was a lot of conversation: "We don't want to hurt you. We have no intention of hurting you." Some of it was about the war in Vietnam; that this is not a good war, and that we shouldn't be there. One of them said: "You send the boys away to be killed." Father Philip Berrigan told me he didn't want to hurt me, and I am sure he meant it.

DEFENSE. Can you remember this having been said: "Don't fight." "We don't mean you any bodily harm." "You are helping in the deaths of American boys"?

WITNESS. That is right. Yes, I remember that. sir.

DEFENSE. When you speak of an injury you received, would that be an injury for which you treated yourself with a Band-Aid?

WITNESS. Well, I went to the doctor, really, because it was—I suppose . . . was, maybe, superficial. But I was very, very, very, very much upset. Mental anguish, I had.

DEFENSE. Would you conceive that the prime purpose of the files, and the work you do, is to serve the government?

WITNESS. Yes, sir. The Army of Defense. I am part of the Army of Defense.

DEFENSE. Mrs. Boyle, did not some of the defendants while in jail send you flowers and candy?

PROSECUTION. Objection, Your Honor.

JUDGE. Strike it out. We are not trying the manners of the defendants, neither their good manners nor their bad manners. We are trying a specific charge.

DEFENSE. No more questions. (*Crosses back to desk.*) We agree with the government that the defendants did participate in the burning of the records.

(WITNESS *exits.*)

DANIEL BERRIGAN. (*Moving* D.) Yes, we agree with the government on the facts up to a point. We offer now our testimony—uttered in the courtroom but not in courtroom order. (DARST *crosses to* R. *witness rail.*) So in our order, this is how they were burned, as David Darst described it: (DANIEL BERRIGAN *crosses* D. L.)

DAVID DARST. We made a very crude form of napalm. We didn't use all the ingredients called for. Ours consisted of two parts gasoline, one part soap flakes. Nor did we cook our mix into a jelly. We left it in liquid form so we could pour it on the files. We made it from a formula in the Green Beret Handbook published by the School for Special Warfare at Fort Bragg.

DEFENSE. Mr. Darst, will you tell us what your role was at Catonsville?

DAVID DARST. I was not actually in the room when the files were taken. Perhaps I could be called the lookout man at Catonsville.

DEFENSE. Lookout man?

DAVID DARST. Well, if anyone came to stop us I was to hurry in and let the others know. You might call it a Bonnie and Clyde act on behalf of God and man.

(MARY MOYLAN *crosses to* L. *witness rail.* DAVID DARST *returns to seat,* U. R. DANIEL BERRIGAN *crosses* U. L.)

DANIEL BERRIGAN. We agreed with the government on the facts up to a point. But the end of theirs was only the beginning of ours.

DEFENSE. Miss Moylan: will you tell us something about your background?

MARY MOYLAN. I was born and raised here in Baltimore. My father was a reporter at the courthouse across the street. I went to Mercy Hospital of Nursing and graduated from there. I also attended the Johns Hopkins School of Midwifery. Then I helped found the Women Volunteers Association, a Catholic lay group that places qualified women for service in Africa—

JUDGE. Africa?

MARY MOYLAN. Yes, Your Honor. All of us here have worked to better human conditions at home and abroad. (THOMAS MELVILLE *crosses to* C. *witness rail.*) I went to Uganda in 1959— (*Returns to seat.*)

THOMAS MELVILLE. —Born in Boston, Massachusetts, in 1930. My father was supervisor of a chain of food stores and during World War II he ran a war plant. My youngest brother was a Marine Corps helicopter pilot and is now in the Marine Reserves.

DEFENSE. Are you married, Mr. Melville?

THOMAS MELVILLE. To Marjorie Melville, a defendant in this case. (MARJORIE MELVILLE *crosses to* L. *witness rail.*) We met when she was a nun and I was a priest of the Maryknoll Order and we were working in Guatemala—

PROSECUTION. (*Fretfully*.) Guatemala—

MARJORIE MELVILLE. —and were married in January of this year. My father was an American working in Mexico, where I was born. (JOHN HOGAN *crosses to* R. *witness rail*.) I went to the American school in Mexico City and then to high school in El Paso and later I went to Webster College in St. Louis. I got my degree at Maryknoll, New York—

JOHN HOGAN. —and I had always thought of going into the Navy myself, since my father and brother both had been in the Navy, but . . . during my senior year in high school in New Haven I felt . . . I wanted to find a community in which I could be working with my hands, physical work . . . and I became interested in joining the Maryknoll Brothers. They finally accepted me. (MELVILLES *return to seats*.) I had training in carpentry and other trades. In 1961 I was assigned to Guatemala . . . working on a hospital the Brothers were building . . . and later assigned to work on a farm cooperative project—the Pope John Colony it was called, with Father Melville.

DEFENSE. (*Crosses nearer* HOGAN.) You are referring to the defendant, Thomas Melville, Mr. Hogan?

JOHN HOGAN. Yes, sir. We were helping the Indians clear a jungle area, reclaim it.

DEFENSE. You were teaching them to reclaim land?

JOHN HOGAN. Which they were supposed to receive the ownership of, but this turned out to be an impossibility. But at the time I felt it was an opportunity to be useful, because I was working—it was cooperative work and it made for the spirit of the place. We were teaching the people how they could work together to achieve a great project—and I was working for Tom Melville, a priest who did not have a paternalistic attitude with the people.

PROSECUTION. Your Honor, I wonder if we can get to the point, the real issue.

(DAVID DARST *crosses to* C. *witness rail*.)

DEFENSE. I am trying to bring this gentleman to what brought him to go to Catonsville.

PROSECUTION. We need to get to the real meat of the thing.

(JOHN HOGAN *returns to seat*.)

DAVID DARST. —Going from Memphis, Tennessee, where I was born to St. Mary's College in Winona, Minnesota, where I graduated summa cum laude. My father was a lieutenant-colonel in the Corps of Engineers, U. S. Army, in World War II. (GEORGE MISCHE *crosses to* R. *witness rail*.) I have brothers at Harvard, Yale and Notre Dame and was myself scheduled to go to Harvard Divinity School on a scholarship, but this was interrupted—

PROSECUTION. Your Honor—

DEFENSE. Briefly, Mr. Mische—

GEORGE MISCHE. —Born in St. Cloud, Minnesota, and am thirty-two years of age, married, with a six-and-a-half-month-old baby daughter and another on the way. . . . My wife is in the courtroom. My father came to this country from Germany at the age of 19 and became a labor organizer. He got involved in programs concerned with the working class. Later he became supervisor of attendance at the veterans' hospital in St. Cloud. I have four brothers. One started a Catholic Worker place in Chicago in the skid row area. It is still going in Chicago.

PROSECUTION. I don't think any of this is relevant—

GEORGE MISCHE. I think it is, Your Honor. My father coming home from that veterans' hospital and telling us stories about the treatment of the patients—it made an impression on me. These men left over from World War I and World War II, who did not enjoy the same thing I did at home, of having a regular family life but were condemned to these types of hospitals for the rest of their lives—it had a profound, let's say, impression on all of our family. And my brothers working with the blacks and the poor—it was very much the ethic of our family that there was something more important in the world than just your own survival. You just couldn't get hung up on getting your own color TV set. When you got out, you did not go out to seek money, you went out to find your own world, to see what you could contribute to your God, and your fellow men and your country.

JUDGE. If you are through, Mr. Mische—

GEORGE MISCHE. No, sir.

JUDGE. (*To* DEFENSE.) We must urge Counsel: the defendants must come closer to Catonsville.

DEFENSE. I am trying to accelerate, Your Honor.

GEORGE MISCHE. In the peace movement one of the most powerful things I knew of was Philip Berrigan's first trial for the blood pouring. A six-year sentence for pouring blood on draft files.

(*Gavel.* GEORGE MISCHE *returns to seat and* THOMAS LEWIS *replaces him at* C. *witness rail.*)

THOMAS LEWIS. I was head of the art department at Archbishop Curley High School here in Baltimore, and teaching classes in the inner city—the ghetto areas—and continuing to paint—

JUDGE. We are not trying you as an artist, Mr. Lewis.

THOMAS LEWIS. I consider that aspect of myself important here, Your Honor. But what I was going to say is that I lost all my teaching jobs with the exception of my ghetto teaching when I acted at the Baltimore Customs House last October. Four of us poured blood on the Selective Service records. Human blood and animal blood, and most of the human blood was Phil Berrigan's—

JUDGE. We are not trying that case, Mr. Lewis.

DANIEL BERRIGAN. (*Standing, as* PHILIP BERRIGAN *crosses to* C. *witness rail and* THOMAS LEWIS *returns to seat.*) My brother looks tired. Brought here he and Tom Lewis in handcuffs. They keep him in a cellblock with twelve other men.

DEFENSE. (*To* PHILIP BERRIGAN.) Father Berrigan, what is your current clerical status and work?

PHILIP BERRIGAN. Currently I suppose I have some sort of ministry within the Federal prison system. I am presently incarcerated in the Federal Prison Camp at Allenwood.

DANIEL BERRIGAN. (*Crosses* D. L.) Phil was the first priest in the country to be tried for a political crime and be convicted. I have always thought my brother to be one of the most fearless of men. If you think this is bias, well, others have thought so too.

PHILIP BERRIGAN. All of us, there were six brothers, were born in Minnesota. My father was railroading out there and he married my mother, who was a German immigrant. Minnesota was still pioneer country. We lived on the Iron Range. It was a struggle to survive the bitter winters. We were poor. I remember the depression years very well. I think this is true of my brother Dan as well. I remember my mother putting up people from the road; there were many men traveling the roads then who were impoverished and desperate. Even though we did not have too much to eat she would never refuse them.

DANIEL BERRIGAN. (*Crosses* D. R. *to steps.*) We were obsessed by poverty. I remember my mother being sick with TB, hospitalized for over a year, and my Aunt Maggie, my father's spinster sister, keeping house for us. She starved us: bread and butter sandwiches, molasses cookies. What a scene! I know that made revolutionaries out of us. Every Sunday we'd go to see Mom at the hospital and she'd look at those six pale, thin little faces and cry out in sorrow. The doctors were pessimistic about my mother surviving, but she recovered out of sheer will power in order to get the witch out of the house.

PHILIP BERRIGAN. And all six boys went to parochial school about two miles away. We had to walk both ways and pack our lunches. We were educated by nuns in a rather . . . well . . . harsh and authoritarian environment.

DEFENSE. (*Crosses up onto stage near* R. *witness rail.*) Now, as I understand it, you spent several years involved in the war effort in Europe, particularly in—

PHILIP BERRIGAN. I would just like to say something very factual about that. I was an enthusiastic participant in World War II and our country's war effort in contrast of course to my present attitude . . .

DANIEL BERRIGAN. Phil was decorated and commissioned in the field, while I was tucked away in a seminary in the Maryland hills. War raised no questions among us seminarians: we were kept immune from the facts of modern war . . . (*Crosses down offstage and returns to seat* U. R.)

DEFENSE. What happened after your discharge from military service?

PHILIP BERRIGAN. I entered the Society of Saint Joseph for training toward the priesthood.

DEFENSE. Could you tell us what the Society is?

PHILIP BERRIGAN. The Society of Saint Joseph is an order dedicated to the service of the American black man, which began to operate in this country shortly after the Civil War.

DEFENSE. What, by the way, is your standing in the order since the Catonsville episode?

PHILIP BERRIGAN. Well, I think my superiors went through some sort of cultural shock.

PROSECUTION. What his superiors went through is irrelevant.

PHILIP BERRIGAN. I am still in good standing.

DEFENSE. What led you to join this order, Father?

PHILIP BERRIGAN. I think it was what I saw of the conditions of black people when I was in military training in the South. One time when we were out on maneuvers we happened to be trying out the rations that would be fed us overseas. It was very hot and we were famished. At the end of the day we came upon some black people who were selling whole chickens for one dollar apiece. Five or six of us bought chickens and ravenously ate them. Then a white boy came along, grinned at us. Said we had been eating not chicken but buzzard.

PROSECUTION. (*Crosses up to* JUDGE.) Your Honor, the defendant is not getting to the question and issue in this case.

PHILIP BERRIGAN. I tell that story to illustrate not only the poverty—

DEFENSE. (*Crosses back to seat.*) Sometimes the issues are not as clearly defined as the prosecutor would wish.

PROSECUTION. And background is only background.

JUDGE. I think the issue could be proved more quickly.

(PROSECUTION *crosses back to seat.*)

PHILIP BERRIGAN. (*To* PROSECUTION.) I am trying to say what it means to be black in this country. After ordination I went to New Orleans to teach in a black high school. We also worked with the poor in the slums of New Orleans. We tried to provide a bridge between the black and the white communities. We tried to attack racism at its roots. We tried to open minds a bit—

JUDGE. We are not trying the racial situation in the United States, nor are we trying the high moral charac-ter of this witness.

PHILIP BERRIGAN. Your Honor, I see that racial situ-ation as leading me straight to the pouring of blood on draft records and—

JUDGE. We are not hearing that case—

PHILIP BERRIGAN. (*Riding through.*) —and then on to Catonsville, to bear witness first by blood and then by fire.

(*Gavel.* PHILIP BERRIGAN *returns to seat.* MARY MOYLAN *crosses to* R. *witness rail.*)

MARY MOYLAN. For me, the political turning point in my life came while I was in Uganda. I was working as a nurse midwife with the White Sisters of Africa at Fort

Portal up near the Mountains of the Moon. While I was in Uganda, American planes began bombing the Congo and we were very close to the Congo border. The planes came over and bombed two villages in Uganda, supposedly by accident. What were American planes, piloted by emigré Cubans, doing bombing in the Congo anyway? As far as I knew, the United Nations was the peacekeeping force in the Congo. Where the hell did the American planes come in? If you will excuse the language, Your Honor. This made me very interested in our foreign policy.

DEFENSE. And under what circumstances did you leave Uganda?

MARY MOYLAN. A serious conflict finally developed between myself and the Administrator of Hospitals. I said I loved Fort Portal very much and that I was seriously thinking about renewing my contract, but that there were several things I must object to. It was becoming obvious to me that the present setup of missions was largely irrelevant and not able to take part in the changes that were necessary in the African countries. I felt that the Africans should have more responsibility. Much of our role seemed to be to provide a white face in the black community.

JUDGE. We are not trying the situation in Africa, Miss Moylan; we have a specific charge.

MARY MOYLAN. I was fired and asked to leave, but I stayed on in Uganda for a while to explain—

PROSECUTION. I would suggest again we get to the issues to be determined and quicken the pace.

DEFENSE. Sometimes it cannot be quickened, sir.

JUDGE. (*To* DEFENSE.) But we must try.

DEFENSE. Miss Moylan, would you relate your experience in Africa to what you found when you came back to the United States?

MARY MOYLAN. Of all that happened to me in Africa the instance which is most indelibly printed on my mind was the bombing by American planes. I came home to Washington, D.C., and had to deal with the scene there:

the insanity and the brutality of the cops and the type of life that was led by most of the citizens of that city—seventy per cent black. Nobody believed that cops were ever brutal; all black people just happened to be lippy and they needed to get a slap in the face once in a while and that was just a fact of life. (GEORGE MISCHE *crosses to* C. *witness rail*.) I found it to be just like our politicans say: our foreign policy is, indeed, a reflection of our domestic policy. (*Crosses back to seat*.)

GEORGE MISCHE. I went down to Yucatan, down to Central America, for the Alliance for Progress, going with the idea that the Latins would be waiting at the boat to greet me because I was an American. This is the naiveté we have, I guess, until we arrive overseas. We were not only not welcome, we had bricks thrown at us. This confused me, but after I became involved I started to understand why bricks were thrown at us. We were working in two countries where revolutions had taken place. I should not say "revolutions"; I should say "coups d'état," military overthrow of governments. Two democratically elected governments were overthrown by the military with Pentagon support. Our programs were . . . (*Crossing toward jury*.) Let me give you an example of what was going on. There was a specific program called the American Institute for Free Labor Development. The idea was, it came out of the University of Chicago, but later on we realized it was a CIA front—

JUDGE. We are not trying the CIA, Mr. Mische—

GEORGE MISCHE. At that point I felt I could not in conscience go on with this work, because John Kennedy had said we would not deal with military dictatorships. At the overthrow of democracy we would stop all military support and all economic support. We would withdraw our people to force the leaders to return to democracy. Well, when I saw the opposite occur I resigned. This reversal of things had most impact on me in the Dominican Republic.

JUDGE. We are not—

GEORGE MISCHE. (*Riding through.*) —That was such a tragedy as to be unbelievable.

DEFENSE. (*Quickly: forestalling* JUDGE, *who is about to speak sharply.*) Mr. Mische, after you left the Alliance for Progress, what did you do?

GEORGE MISCHE. I came back to the United States and in my trusty Chevrolet I traveled 75,000 miles in a year and a half. I went around this country. I talked to university students, I talked to religious groups, I talked to businessmen's clubs, I spoke to 80 Catholic bishops. As a Catholic I apologize to you for their cowardice.

PROSECUTION. Your Honor, may I object?

JUDGE. We are not trying the Catholic bishops of the United States.

GEORGE MISCHE. Unfortunately I asked them, since they have 80 billion dollars' worth of property and ten times as much in investments, if they were really to live in the spirit of the stable in which Christ was born, then why not get rid of the buildings, give them to the poor . . .

PROSECUTION. Your Honor, I do not want to keep standing up and objecting.

GEORGE MISCHE. I am telling you my background.

PROSECUTION. It is irrelevant.

JUDGE. It is not testimony. It is argument. It has nothing to do with testimony, what he has been saying. It is arguing the case. This is not the time or the place for argument.

(GEORGE MISCHE *returns to seat.* THOMAS MELVILLE *crosses to* L. *witness rail.*)

DEFENSE. Father Melville, what was it you saw in Guatemala that caused you to change your conception of your role as a priest? When did you go there, by the way?

THOMAS MELVILLE. I went to Guatemala in August of 1957. I was not there very long when I felt I was getting a little ahead of myself. The material circumstances of the people—I hesitate to use the word "poverty"; they were living in utter misery. So I thought perhaps instead of talking about the life to come and justice beyond perhaps I could do a little to ameliorate their conditions on this earth and at the same time give a demonstration of what Christianity is all about.

MARJORIE MELVILLE. (*Crosses to* R. *witness rail.*) We were trying to find out our role as Christians. Was it to see people's needs and get involved or were we to say, "Well, this is too difficult. It is too hard to know what to do"? Do we stand back or do we go in on the side of the people and say, "What can I do to help?"

THOMAS MELVILLE. I put up the title of the church property so that a cooperative could get a loan. I got into trouble because I signed the loan myself, without the permission of the bishops. There was simply no organization in the country that would help the people. I know you are bored by this . . .

JUDGE. No one is bored by this: it is an extremely interesting story. However, we cannot try the last ten years in Guatemala.

DEFENSE. Your Honor, I think you will find a very close relationship between the past experiences of the defendants and their action at Catonsville.

THOMAS MELVILLE. Perhaps I can just say that we were back in this country only one month when we participated at Catonsville. So what happened to us in Guatemala is, I feel, very relevant.

JUDGE. Well, you are perfectly entitled to explain that. I just did not understand the connection.

MARJORIE MELVILLE. I had been living a very sheltered life in Guatemala City, teaching at the "Maryknoll Hilton," as the rich ladies called it—these were the people I was dealing with. Then I took a course in Christian social doctrine. I went into the slum areas. I began to understand what life in Guatemala was all about. The group of students I was working with chose a name which in English means "crater," because they felt that our spirit should be like a volcano which erupts forth love for men. At the crater we began to work with the peasants. But every time we asked for help for very simple projects like setting up a cooperative or putting water in a village we found that American funds were not available. But American money was available for the purchase of new police cars for the secret police. It came out that two thousand new policemen were being trained by us in Guatemala and the uniforms, salaries, food—the whole thing—was being paid for by us.

THOMAS MELVILLE. Under one government, land that belonged to the United Fruit Company was bought and distributed to peasants. But a later President, Castillo Armas, took the land from the peasants and gave it back to the United Fruit Company. Eisenhower later admitted our involvement. There were about three thousand people who did not want to move off the land. They were killed or moved forcibly.

JUDGE. We are not trying the United Fruit Company.

THOMAS MELVILLE. Castillo Armas was later assassinated.

MARJORIE MELVILLE. I had been really so proud to be an American when I went down there, Your Honor. Maybe it was because I was born abroad but I grew up to have a great love for my country. But in Guatemala it was really a shock to me to realize my country was not exactly the great ideal I had always pictured. It might sound silly, but I think it was a little bit like a child's discovery that Santa Claus does not exist and that all those gifts are not from him at all. All that I had thought about my country—well, it was not as beautiful as I had expected.

THOMAS MELVILLE. Our ambassador, our military attaché, our naval attaché were all recently assassinated and I would think that people in this country would begin to wonder.

JUDGE. We are trying a specific charge. We just can't worry here about Guatemala.

THOMAS MELVILLE. Eighty-five per cent of the people in Guatemala live in misery. You don't live in misery; perhaps that is why you don't worry about it. They live in misery because two per cent of the population are determined to keep them that way. The United States Government identifies its interests in Guatemala with the Guatemalan two per cent who control the country. So if the peasant movement does not conduct itself according to their wishes—that is to say if such a movement is not completely ineffective—they start screaming, "They are Communists!" and begin executing these people.

JUDGE. You mean to say that the United States Government is executing Guatemalans?

THOMAS MELVILLE. (*Crosses to* JUDGE.) Yes, Your Honor.

JUDGE. Has the United States Government sent troops into Guatemala?

(MARJORIE MELVILLE *crosses to* C. *witness rail.*)

THOMAS MELVILLE. Yes, Your Honor.

JUDGE. When?

THOMAS MELVILLE. At the end of 1966 and in January of 1967.

JUDGE. And you say that the United States is executing people there?

THOMAS MELVILLE. (*Crosses to* C. *witness rail.*) Yes. It was reported even in *Time* magazine.

JUDGE. Well, we are not trying the series of Guatemalan revolutions.

(DEFENSE *sits.*)

THOMAS MELVILLE. We wanted to participate in the Guatemalan revolution. Myself, Marjorie, who was still a nun at the time, John Hogan and five others agreed to join the revolutionaries, because we knew that it would not look good for the United States if an American priest

or nun were killed in Guatemala by American Green
Berets. We wanted to complicate things for the United
States in Guatemala, because we did not want to see a
slaughter there like the one in Vietnam.

MARJORIE MELVILLE. Our superiors got a little nervous
about our desire to work with the peasants and they
thought it would be better if we left the country before
the thing got too big. So we were asked to leave . . .

JOHN HOGAN. (*Overlap.*) We were expelled and I—

JUDGE. (*Under.*) Mr. Hogan!

PROSECUTION. (*Under.*) We need to get to the issue—

JOHN HOGAN. (*Riding through.*) —I was going to say
. . . I hated to leave because I had gotten to love the
people very much.

(*Pause.*)

THOMAS MELVILLE. In December of 1967 we went to
Mexico trying to help—

PROSECUTION. Mexico!

THOMAS MELVILLE. —trying to help the peasant and
student leaders who also had been expelled. Their lives
were in danger.

JUDGE. We cannot—

(*Gavel.* GEORGE MISCHE, *booming over gavel, crosses to*
R. *witness rail.* MARSHALS *edge in.*)

GEORGE MISCHE. Where it was most terrible, Your
Honor, was in the Dominican Republic. A man like
Trujillo ran that country for thirty-two years. When
someone dared talk about social change or social reform
they would go into his house, take the head of the family
out of the house, cut off his penis, put it in his mouth,
cut off his arms and legs, drop them in the doorway.

PROSECUTION. I have to object. I am trying to be
patient—

GEORGE MISCHE. (*Crossing toward jury, stopping at*

L. *witness rail*.) I am trying to speak as a human being to the jury who, I hope, are human beings and can understand us.

JUDGE. Mr. Mische! (*Pause. And then, as if surmounting the need to reprimand, to say something more compelling*.) We are not here to try the history of the world in the twentieth century.

GEORGE MISCHE. *We* are dealing with the history of the United States—

JUDGE. If this witness insists on arguing his case, I may have to take steps to stop it. (MISCHE *and* MELVILLES *return to seats.* MARSHALS *cross up behind set.* DAVID DARST *crosses to* L. *witness rail*.) From now on I will allow only testimony that leads narrowly and directly to that act of civil disobedience at Catonsville.

DAVID DARST. I will try to say it clearly, Your Honor. Two years ago I was teaching high school for the first time. Many of the boys were facing imminent induction. I began to feel it was my duty to cry out. One of the things I did was to send back my own draft card to my board. But they gave me a clerical deferment, and then drafted me as a Christian Brother. I thought, well, good, I will refuse this and thus perhaps raise a cry. But only my friends knew about this. Thus it was not a cry. Later on I was prosecuted for this failure to report for induction and a trial was set, but the government somewhat mysteriously and, I feel, somewhat cowardly, dropped the charges just before the trial was to begin—

PROSECUTION. I object to that characterization of the government.

JUDGE. Do you claim to be a conscientious objector?

DAVID DARST. I asked to be considered a specific objector to this war.

JUDGE. At any rate, the charges were dropped.

DAVID DARST. I was trying to make a cry, Your Honor—

JUDGE. We are not trying the draft card case, Mr. Darst.

PROSECUTION. Mr. Darst, you have said elsewhere that draft files have no right to exist and this justifies your burning them.

DAVID DARST. Yes, sir.

PROSECUTION. Do you believe that slum properties have no right to exist?

DAVID DARST. Slum properties I would say have no right to exist.

PROSECUTION. Would you symbolically burn down slum properties?

DAVID DARST. How could I symbolically burn down slum properties?

(DAVID DARST *returns to seat and* THOMAS LEWIS *crosses to* R. *witness rail*.)

DEFENSE. Mr. Lewis, you are an artist—

JUDGE. We have said we are not trying him as an artist.

THOMAS LEWIS. Of course, on an artist the visual impact of the war is immediate, Your Honor. Let me speak of an experience that has bearing on why I am here. Some years ago I went to do some sketches at a civil rights demonstration here in Baltimore. They had just arrested some clergymen. You know I had a feeling I should be where they were. I picketed for a while. It is a shocking thing, walking a picket line for the first time, sensing the hostility of the people, the white people particularly, when we went to suburbia to demonstrate for open occupancy.

JUDGE. We are not trying the issue of open occupancy. You must—

THOMAS LEWIS. I'm getting there, Your Honor. In Christianity we are taught that all men are a human family. Yet I was not profoundly moved about Vietnam until my younger brother was there. The war helped educate me. A group of us began what we called the Interfaith Peace Mission of Baltimore. We began with a peace vigil. We prayed for peace. We followed this with a walk. We had visits with Maryland congressmen and senators. We wrote letters to them. We met with silence, with hostility and apathy. One of the vigils in Washington was at the home of Dean Rusk. Rusk said it was not his job to deal with moral matters. He said to the clergymen in the group that it was their responsibility to deal with the morality of the war. Well, we did not need his homilies. We had been doing that for years. So we turned toward the military. There was no response. They accepted no responsibility for the direction of the war. The responsibility was not theirs. They were just obeying orders.

PROSECUTION. You said "no response." You mean they did not do what you asked them to do, is that it?

THOMAS LEWIS. No response. We were standing there. We were speaking to them as Americans. We were proud to be Americans. Yet we have representatives in Vietnam who do terrible things in our name. We were saying to the military, "This is wrong. This is immoral. This is illegal." And their response to this was, they were only obeying orders.

PROSECUTION. But they did respond to you, did they not?

THOMAS LEWIS. It was an atrocious response. (PHILIP BERRIGAN *rises, crosses to* LEWIS.) Out of all of this we came to civil disobedience. We made a decision to protest. This protest would involve the pouring of blood—

JUDGE. I have said we are not trying that case—

PHILIP BERRIGAN. (*Crossing to* C. *witness rail.*) We are trying to explain our act as Christians, Your Honor. Our act came from the Christian roots of protest. We took our own blood—Reverend Mengel, Dave Eberhart, Tom Lewis, and myself. We attempted to anoint these files with the Christian symbol of life and purity, which is blood, in order to illustrate our horror over blood being shed in Vietnam—American and Vietnamese blood.

THOMAS LEWIS. Not only American but Vietnamese. Blood in biblical terms and in contemporary terms is a symbol of reconciliation. (*Beat.*) Your Honor—

(*Silence.*)

DEFENSE. (*Crossing up near* LEWIS.) In that action all of you known as the Baltimore Four were convicted and so it was while awaiting sentence that you and Phil Berrigan undertook the action at Catonsville. My question is: why did you do this while a sentence was staring you in the face—knowing that it would be the greater for engaging in this second act—and this second act would subject you to still another sentence?

THOMAS LEWIS. There was a difference in our minds between the two protests. The draft records on which we poured blood were records of the inner city, the ghetto areas. Part of that protest was to dramatize that the war is taking more cannon fodder from the poor areas than from the more affluent areas. The symbolism was perhaps clearer in the second case. At Catonsville we used a contemporary symbol—napalm—which has been used in South America as well as Vietnam. The United States makes it. It is part of our foreign aid. At Catonsville we used this symbol to destroy records which are potential death certificates. They stand for the death of men, they represent men who are put in the situation where they have to kill. But beyond this, napalm manufactured in the United States is part of our foreign aid. We supply weaponry to more than eighty countries. We have troops in more than forty countries. These troops are backed up with our weaponry. The fact is, the American system can flourish only if we expand our economy. The fact is we produce more goods than we are capable of consuming. We must have new markets. We must bring our industries, our way of life, into Vietnam and Latin America. We must protect our interests there. But we asked at Catonsville, "Whose interests are these? Who represents the interests of Vietnam?"

PROSECUTION. Did you consider that others might have a view about Vietnam that was contrary to yours?

THOMAS LEWIS. I don't meet any of them in prison.

(DEFENSE *returns to seat.* PROSECUTION *crosses to top step beside his desk.*)

PROSECUTION. Yes or no, were you aware—that has been the question, the only question, to all the defendants, from the beginning—were you aware that it was against the law to take records from the Selective Service and burn them?

THOMAS LEWIS. I wasn't concerned with the law. I wasn't even thinking about the law. I went in there with the intent of stopping what the files justify. The young men whose files we destroyed have not yet been drafted, may not be drafted, may not be sent to Vietnam for cannon fodder. My intent in going in there was to save lives. A person may break the law to save lives.

JUDGE. If these men were not sent, other people would have been sent, who would not otherwise have been sent, would they not?

THOMAS LEWIS. But why, Your Honor? Why this? Why does it have to be like this? You are accepting the fact that if these men are not sent other men will be sent. You are not even asking what can be done to stop the insane killing— You are accepting this insane killing, Your Honor, as in Nazi Germany people accepted the massacre of other people. This is insane and I protest this.

PROSECUTION. I move that all of this be stricken. I don't know how long he is going to continue.

THOMAS LEWIS. How long? I have six years, Mr. Prosecutor, I have lots of time.

(LEWIS *"freezes."* MARSHALS *exit.* DANIEL BERRIGAN *crosses* D. C. *into a SPECIAL LIGHT.*)

DANIEL BERRIGAN. The world expects—these are the words of Camus—the world expects that Christians will speak out loud and clear so that never a doubt, never the slightest doubt, could arise in the heart of the simplest man. The world expects that Christians will get away from abstractions and confront the bloodstained face which history has taken on today. The grouping we need is a grouping of men resolved to speak up clearly and pay up personally. (*Beat*. THOMAS LEWIS *and* PHILIP BER- RIGAN *move* U. *as* GEORGE MISCHE *crosses to* C. *witness rail*.) We'd like to tell you now how we came together for Catonsville. Tom Lewis was ready when Phil put the question to him and George Mische came in right after. (*Crosses down off platform* R.)

DEFENSE. Mr. Mische: couldn't you have done some- thing less drastic about these problems than burning draft files? Why did you feel compelled to act at Catonsville?

GEORGE MISCHE. I have a strong feeling about what happened in Germany in the last war. I mentioned that my father was from Germany. The United States in 1945 supported the Nuremberg trials. I thought that was the finest precedent this country ever set. I said: good; you are righ. Every German citizen had the responsibility to stop Hitler. If that was true then, and I thought it was, then it was also true that this is expected of me now as a Christian—and also expected of our Jewish brothers— to stop the atrocity of the war in Vietnam.

JUDGE. Counsel—

DEFENSE. Yes. The question is: couldn't you have done something less drastic, like picketing or writing to your congressmen and so on?

GEORGE MISCHE. Well, first of all, I have done all of those other things. I have been doing those things for years. I felt that the crisis needed something drastic, something people could see. There is a higher law we are commanded to obey. It takes precedence over human laws. My intent was to follow the higher law. My intent was to save lives; to stop the madness: that was my in- tent in going to Catonsville. My intent was . . . (*Beat*.) I am trying to say that the style of one's actions must coincide with the style of his life. And that is all.

(GEORGE MISCHE *moves* U. *as* MARY MOYLAN *crosses to* C. *witness rail*.)

MARY MOYLAN. You know, as a nurse, your profession is to preserve life, to prevent disease. To a nurse, the effect of napalm on human beings is apparent. Think of children and women bombed by napalm, burned alive by a substance which does not roll off. It is a jelly; it adheres; it continues burning. This is inhuman, absolutely. To pour napalm on pieces of paper is certainly preferable to using it on human beings. When you see the imperative put on you—

DEFENSE. (*Interrupting.*) What imperative?

MARY MOYLAN. That you act on what you say you believe. This is what it means to be a Christian. This is what Christ meant when He lived. We have not only to talk, but if we see something wrong we have to be willing to do something about it. This is my belief. What I really wanted to do—what I was saying by pouring napalm on draft files is that I wish to celebrate life, not engage in a dance of death.

JUDGE. It would be to do what?

THOMAS LEWIS. (*Taking one step forward.*) I was saving my soul. I had a choice between saving my soul and losing it.

(MARY MOYLAN *moves* U. *as the* MELVILLES *and* HOGAN *cross to* C. *witness rail.*)

PROSECUTION. Mr. Melville, in fact for your wife and yourself, the basic motivation for going to Catonsville and burning the files was not Vietnam but American interference in Guatemala, isn't that right?

THOMAS MELVILLE. No.

PROSECUTION. That is not right?

THOMAS MELVILLE. No. We came to certain conclusions in Guatemala, and applied them very personally to the people of Guatemala. But we feel just as deeply about what we are doing in Vietnam.

MARJORIE MELVILLE. There comes a moment when you decide that some things should not be . . . and you have to act to try to stop these things.

JOHN HOGAN. If there were a group of children walking along the street, returning home from school, and a car came down the street out of control—even though there was a driver in that car, if I could divert the car from crashing into those children, I would feel an obligation to turn the car from its path. And I know too that if I were driving that car I would hope and pray to God that somebody would smash the car so that I might not destroy those children.

DEFENSE. Mr. Hogan, if you could sum up your intent in going to Catonsville, how would you express it?

JOHN HOGAN. I just want to let people live. That is all.

JUDGE. I did not hear it.

JOHN HOGAN. I said I want to let people live. That is all.

DANIEL BERRIGAN. David Darst came in, leaving his studies at St. Louis University, his Harvard future and looking so clean-cut he was thought to be a plant.

(MELVILLES *and* HOGAN *join the* U. *group as* DAVID DARST *crosses to* C. *witness rail.*)

DAVID DARST. To stop the machine I saw moving and killing, to hinder the war effort in an actual, physical, literal way. To raise a cry, an outcry over what I saw as a very, very clear crime . . .

JUDGE. Did he say crime?

DAVID DARST. Clearly a crime—a clear and wanton slaughter. We have not been able to let sacred life and total death live together quietly within us. My thinking is part of an ethic found in the New Testament that has always drawn the line between people and things. It says that material things are for the use of people, but that people are sacred; they are absolutely ends in themselves, they cannot be used as means. Our point is that we were destroying property at the draft board which is desecrating the most sacred property—life.

(DAVID DARST *moves* U.)

PHILIP BERRIGAN. We do not consider ourselves as having committed a crime.

PROSECUTION. You are going to have to explain, please, how you distinguish violating the law from having committed a crime.

PHILIP BERRIGAN. (*Crosses to* C. *witness rail.*) Yes, we violated the law, but the law is no absolute to us. I must say that our intention was to destroy the files, but our motive was to illustrate genocide in Vietnam and corruption at home. The real issue is: how can men serve love and war? The fact is, they can't. Most Americans have great difficulty seeing the I, the self, as being, the we, humanity. We cannot feel the effects of our actions as others see us. We think we can rape a people and have them love us. We cannot ravage the ecology of Indochina, kill ten civilians for every soldier, and expect anything but do-or-die opposition. We cannot fight the abstraction of Communism by killing the people who believe in it. We cannot talk peace while our deeds give the lie to our words. We can't have it both ways. The point at issue for us personally when we went to Catonsville was not leniency or punishment, not being a danger to the community or a benefit to it, but what it means to be a democratic man and a Christian man. America can treat us as it wills. If it can find justice for us and for the growing numbers who refuse complicity in *its* crime, then it will show a stamina in accord with its national creed. If it cannot then its cup of violence will fill up . . . and up . . . finally to brim over. And at that mysterious point we defendants will have been proven right in choosing revolution over reform—

JUDGE. Revolution?

PHILIP BERRIGAN. I use the term revolution as it is employed by adherents of the Gospel and students of Gandhi—on the human level. People cannot develop until they change. They cannot grow into humanity, they cannot join the human race, unless they change. Such change is revoution. We hope to continue making a nonviolent contribution to it.

DANIEL BERRIGAN. (*Crosses up onto platform.*) I was the last of the nine who agreed to go to Catonsville. I sat up with Philip through a long night, resisting. (*Beat.*) Suddenly I saw my sweet skin was hiding behind others . . . (*Crosses to* C. *witness rail as other* DEFENDANTS *return to their seats.*)

DEFENSE. Father Berrigan, (*Standing.*) after you were ordained in 1952—

JUDGE. It is too far back—

DANIEL BERRIGAN. It was an important year for me, Your Honor. I was transformed politically, a historic year. We all have come here by different roads and this is mine. I was sent to France as the colonial war in Southeast Asia came to a last act at Dienbienphu. There was an exciting movement in the French Church then known as the worker-priests. A large band of these priests received permission to work in the factories and docks and mines, learning what it was to live *with* the people and not apart from them. They began to understand Christianity anew and tried to translate it anew. But our icebox Pope, Pius XII, dissolved the movement in one swift stroke—

JUDGE. We are not trying the worker-priest movement of France.

DANIEL BERRIGAN. I only meant to say, Your Honor, it radicalized me, gave me a practical vision of the Church as she should be . . . woke me to the evils of colonialism . . . a historic year—

JUDGE. We must move forward—

DANIEL BERRIGAN. In 1961 I turned the altar around and said the Mass in English. The kids and I felt that for the first time in a thousand years we were building community around the altar—

JUDGE. Father Berrigan, we must—

DANIEL BERRIGAN. In 1964, Your Honor, I was invited to South Africa. I had about two weeks of intense exposure to a segregationist police state. At one meeting in Durban I remember the question being raised, "What happens to our children if things go so badly that we have to go to jail?" I remember saying I could not answer that question, not being a citizen of that country, but I could perhaps help by reversing the question, "What happens to us and our children if we do *not* go to jail?" I was coming to realize what it might cost to be a Christian.

JUDGE. (*Muttering.*) 1964—

DANIEL BERRIGAN. I was becoming convinced that the war in Vietnam would inevitably worsen. I felt that a cloud no larger than a man's hand would shortly cover the sky. I began to say no to the war, knowing if I delayed too long, I would never find the courage to say no. Cardinal Spellman was still alive. He had always supported American wars. . . . He believed—I think this states his thought—that the highest expression of faith for an American Christian was to support our military efforts. By his Christmas visits to our troops across the world, particularly in Vietnam, he placed an official seal of approval on our military adventuring.

JUDGE. We are not trying—

DANIEL BERRIGAN. I had to say no to that too. I had to say no to the Church. Finally in the autumn of 1965 I was exiled from the United States to Latin America.

JUDGE. What do you mean, "exiled"?

DANIEL BERRIGAN. Sent out, Your Honor, with no return ticket.

JUDGE. You mean the Government of the United States exiled you?

DANIEL BERRIGAN. No, it was a simple arrangement between the Cardinal and my Jesuit superiors. As one of my friends expressed it, sending me to Latin America was a little like tossing Br'er Rabbit into the briar patch. I visited ten countries in four and a half months. In Mexico a student said to me, "We hate you North Americans with all our hearts, but we know that if you do not make it we all come down, we are all doomed." I felt my conscience being pushed forward—

JUDGE. We are only in 1965. You must come closer to Catonsville.

DANIEL BERRIGAN. Yes, sir. In 1968 an invitation came from the government of North Vietnam. Professor Howard Zinn and myself were invited to Hanoi to bring home three captive American airmen. I think we were the first Americans to undergo an American bombing attack. When the burned draft files were brought into court yesterday as evidence, I could not but recall that I had seen in Hanoi evidence of a very different nature. I saw not boxes of burned papers. . . . I saw parts of human bodies preserved in alcohol, the bodies of children, the hearts and organs and limbs of women—teachers, workers, peasants—bombed in fields and churches and schools and hospitals. It was quite clear to me during three years of air war America had been experimenting upon the bodies of the innocent. We had improved our weapons on their flesh.

JUDGE. He did not see this firsthand. He is telling of things he was told in Hanoi, about some things that were preserved in alcohol.

DANIEL BERRIGAN. French, English, Swedish experts, doctors testified these were actually the bodies whose pictures accompanied the exhibits. The meaning of the air war in the North was deliberate, systematic destruction—

JUDGE. We are not trying the air war in North Vietnam.

DANIEL BERRIGAN. I must protest the effort to discredit me on the stand. I am speaking of what I saw. There is a consistent effort to say that I did not see it.

JUDGE. You can say what you saw, but the best evidence of what some crime commission found is what *they* said, and not a summary that you can give in this court.

DANIEL BERRIGAN. So be it. . . . In any case we brought the flyers home. As a result of the trip to Hanoi and of my brother's act of pouring blood on the draft records I understood the limits of what I had done before and the next step that must come.

DEFENSE. (*Standing.*) And was there anything else that determined you to act at Catonsville?

DANIEL BERRIGAN. Another event. The self-immolation of a high school student in Syracuse, New York, in the spring of 1968. This boy had come to a point of despair about the war. He had gone into the Catholic cathedral, drenched himself with kerosene and immolated himself in the street. He was still living a month later when I visited him in the hospital. I smelled the odor of burning flesh and understood anew what I had seen in Vietnam. The boy was dying in torment, his body like a piece of meat upon a grille. He died shortly thereafter. I felt that my senses had been invaded in a new way. I understood again the power of death in the modern world. This boy's death was being multiplied a thousandfold in the Land of Burning Children. So I went to Catonsville and burned some papers because the burning of children is inhuman and unbearable. I went to Catonsville because I had gone to Hanoi.

JUDGE. You must speak more directly to the issue.

DANIEL BERRIGAN. I went to Catonsville because my brother was a man and I must be a man—

JUDGE. To the specific issue—

DANIEL BERRIGAN. Because I could not go on announcing the Gospel from a pedestal. I was threatened with verbalizing my moral substance out of existence. So I went to Hanoi and then to Catonsville and that is why I am here.

JUDGE. You will tell us exactly why—why you went—exactly . . .

DANIEL BERRIGAN. I did not want the children or the grandchildren of the jury or of the judge to be burned with napalm.

JUDGE. You say your intention was to save these children, of the jury, of myself, when you burned the records? That is what I heard you say. I ask if you meant that.

DANIEL BERRIGAN. I meant that, of course I meant that or I would not say it.

JUDGE. You cannot invent arguments now that you would like to have had in your mind then.

DANIEL BERRIGAN. My intention on that day was to save the innocent from death by fire. Yes, I poured napalm on behalf of the prosecutor's and the judge's and the jury's children and grandchildren. If my way of putting the facts is inadmissible then so be it. But I was trying to be concrete about death, because death is a concrete fact, as I have throughout my life tried to be concrete about the existence of God, who is not an abstraction, but is someone before me for whom I am responsible.

DEFENSE. I ask you, Daniel Berrigan, was your action at Catonsville a way of carrying out your religious beliefs?

JUDGE. I am going to have to instruct the jury that, under the law which is binding on me, and therefore on the jury as well, the fact that he may be following his religious principles is not a defense, if it is found that a crime has indeed been committed.

DANIEL BERRIGAN. May I say, Your Honor, that if my religious belief is not accepted as a substantial part of my action then the action is eviscerated of all meaning and I should be committed for insanity. (*Beat.*)

DEFENSE. Father Berrigan, did you not write a statement on Catonsville?

DANIEL BERRIGAN. A meditation written just before the action.

DEFENSE. Would you read it?

DANIEL BERRIGAN. (*Crosses D. C.*) Our apologies, good friends, for the fracture of good order . . . the burning of paper instead of children . . . the angering of orderlies in the front parlor of the charnel house. We could not, so help us God, do otherwise. For we are sick at heart.

Our hearts give us no rest for thinking of the Land of Burning Children and for thinking of that other Child of whom the poet Luke speaks: "This child is set for the fall and rise of many in Israel, a sign that is spoken against." Small consolation . . . a child born to make trouble and to die for it . . . the First Jew (not the last) to be subject of a "definitive solution." And so we stretch out our hands to our brothers throughout the world. We who are priests to our fellow priests. All of us who act against the law turn to the poor of the world, to the Vietnamese, to the victims, to the soldiers who kill and die for the wrong reasons, for no reason at all, because they were so ordered by the authorities of that public order which is in effect a massive institutionalized disorder. We say: killing is disorder; life and gentleness and community and unselfishness is the only order we recognize. For the sake of that order we risk our liberty, our good name. The time is past when good men can remain silent when obedience can segregate men from public risk, when the poor can die without defense. How many indeed must die before our voices are heard? How many must be tortured, dislocated, starved, maddened? How long must the world's resources be raped in the service of legalized murder? When . . . at what point will you say no to this war? We have chosen to say with the gift of our liberty, if necessary our lives: the violence stops here, the death stops here, the suppression of the truth stops here, this war stops here. Redeem the times! The times are inexpressibly evil. And yet—and yet—the times are inexhaustibly good, solaced by the courage and hope of many. The truth rules . . . Christ is not forsaken. In a time of death . . . some men, the resisters, those who work hardily for social change, preach and embrace the truth. In the jaws of death they proclaim their love of the brethren. We think of such men in the world, in our nation, in the churches, and the stone in our breast is dissolved and we take heart once more.

(DANIEL BERRIGAN *returns to seat.* MARSHALS *reenter.*)

DEFENSE. Nothing further, Your Honor.

JUDGE. Is the government ready to make its final statement?

PROSECUTION. The government is ready, Your Honor. May it please the Court and members of the jury. It is now my responsibility to attempt, in summary fashion, to review with you the evidence that has been produced in this courtroom. First of all, I want it clearly understood that the government is not about to put itself in the position—has not heretofore and is not now—of conducting its policies at the end of a string tied to the consciences of these nine defendants. This trial does not include the issues of the Vietnam conflict. It does not include the issue of whether the United States ought to be in that conflict or out of it. (*Crosses up onto platform.*) The government quite candidly admits that the position these defendants took is reasonable—as to the fact that the war is illegal, that it is immoral, that it is against religious principles, that any reasonable man could take that view. We do not even say that a person has to be insane to have the views that they have. No, we don't say that. But this prosecution is the government's response, the law's response, the people's response, to what the defendants did. And what they did was to take government property and throw flammable material on it and burn it beyond recognition. And that is what this case is about. Suppose you were to acquit these people on the only basis possible, in view of everything they have conceded? Acquit them, that is, although they did those acts with the intention of hindering the Selective Service System and of burning the files and records. Suppose that because of their sincerity, their conscience, their religious convictions, they were entitled to be acquitted in this courtroom? If these people were entitled to be acquitted by virtue of their sincerity and religion and conviction, then, according to the same logic, should not the man who commits any other crime be also entitled to acquittal? We also heard about unpleasant things happening, or about to happen, in other areas of the world. Among these nine defendants, there are four or five justifications floating around. One defendant is upset about one ill in the world, and that justifies his going to Catonsville. Another is upset about another ill in the world, and that justifies his going to Catonsville. And so on. The possibilities are infinite. There could in fact be fifty defendants, each upset about fifty different supposed ills in the world. And each one of them could say: this is why I violated the law. Ladies and gentlemen of the jury, the government has never contended that this country is perfect, that it is without flaw, without ills and problems and failings. To assert that would be absurd. But I would suggest to you that, to the extent that this country has problems, those problems will be solved. We will progress. We will get better. The country will get better. But our problems are not going to be solved by people who deliberately violate our laws, the foundation and support for an ordered and just and civilized society. It is your sworn duty to assert, by finding the defendants guilty, that our problems will not be solved, but will be increased beyond imagining, by people who deliberately violate the law under which we all live.

(PROSECUTION *returns to seat as* DEFENSE *crosses onto stage.*)

DEFENSE. Ladies and gentlemen of the jury. Undoubtedly, a great measure of personal reflection is required, even to begin to appreciate the meaning of this trial for us who participated in it. I must beg your leave to inject a personal note. In law school, I was repeatedly warned never to identify too closely with prospective clients. Perhaps under other circumstances this might be considered sound advice. For myself, I must confess with more pride than I could adequately describe, I have come to love and respect the men and women who stand before this court. The Court has agreed that this is a unique case. It shares the historic meaning of other great contests of law. The trial of Socrates was not merely a question of a man sowing confusion and distrust among the youth of Athens; the trial of Jesus could not be reduced to one of conspiracy against the Empire. In a parallel way, there are overriding issues at stake in this case. In the first place, we agree with the prosecutor. The defendants did participate in the burning of the records. But it is not a question of records which are independent of life. We are not talking about driving licenses or licenses to operate a brewery. We are speaking of one kind of records. No others so directly affect life and death on a mass scale. They affect every mother's son who is registered with any board. These records stand quite literally for life and death to young men. The government has also conceded that it is reasonable to hold the views held by the defendants as to the illegality of this war. This is a concession of such far-reaching legal and political significance, for if it is reasonable for an American to believe that the war is illegal, then it has to be equally reasonable for him to take the necessary steps to stop the illegality. Ultimately you and I and the people in this courtroom are the owners of these Selective Service files. We have entrusted their use to a government agency. But that agency is only our *instrument*. When their use is perverted to destroy innocent life, the files no longer have a right to exist. So we come to the only issue left for you to decide: whether, in your opinion, they are guilty or innocent of crime. I want to point out to you a case which offers parallels to this one, a case which affected the character of American history, some two hundred years ago. The defendant was a printer, Peter Zenger, by name; he was accused of seditious libel. Andrew Hamilton, the defending lawyer, spoke the following words in the course of the trial (and it seems to me they are of point here). He said, and I quote: "Jurors are to see with their own eyes, to hear with their own ears, and to make use of their conscience and understanding in judging of the lives, liberties and estates of their fellow subjects." Ladies and gentlemen of the jury, that is what we are asking you to do.

JUDGE. You are urging the jury to make their decision on the basis of conscience. This morning in chambers I said to you that if you attempt to do this, the Court will interrupt to tell the jury their duty. The jury may not decide this case on the basis of conscience. The jury will decide this case solely on the basis of the facts presented in this courtroom by both sides.

DEFENSE. Ladies and gentlemen of the jury: all the peaceful acts of the defendants . . . all the words, writings, marching, fasting, demonstrating . . . over a period of some years have failed to change a single American decision in Vietnam; failed even momentarily to slow the unnatural, senseless destruction of men, women and children, including the destruction of our own sons. A destruction of our own sons. A destruction wrought in the name of a policy that passes all human understanding. Perhaps in the last analysis this cataclysm of our times can be understood only in the lives of a few men, who for one moment stand naked before the horrified gaze of their fellow men. I am appealing to you, as I imagine Andrew Hamilton appealed to his jury, to consider all the "facts." (*Returns to seat.*)

JUDGE. Ladies and gentlemen of the jury: you are to consider all the facts and the law. The law does not recognize religious conviction or some higher law is justification for commission of a crime, no matter how good the motive may be. The law does not permit jurors to be governed by sympathy, prejudice or public opinion. You are judges of the facts. Your sole duty is to ascertain the truth. The jury may now begin their deliberations. (MARSHALS *usher jury out.* DEFENSE *crosses up to* DE-FENDANTS *to confer.*) Now then, does either the prosecution or the defense wish to take exception to any of the rulings of this Court?

DEFENSE. Your Honor, the defendants have requested to be permitted to speak frankly and openly with the Court.

JUDGE. I want to hear the defendants. I do not want to cut them off from anything they may want to say.

(THOMAS MELVILLE *stands to face* JUDGE. DEFENSE *returns to his seat.* HOGAN *and* LEWIS *stand.*)

THOMAS MELVILLE. Your Honor, after burning the files, we waited for fifteen minutes until the police came, to give public witness to what we did. You have sent the jury out—to judge merely whether we committed the acts which we admitted from the beginning that we had committed. If it is only a question of whether we committed this act or not, we feel it would be better if the jury is dismissed. We can save ourselves a lot of time by receiving an immediate sentence from you.

JUDGE. It is quite true that I have not submitted to the jury the question you would like to have submitted, in a way you would like. But the law limits me in that regard. If you had gone to Catonsville and taken one file under some token arrangement, you might have had something to argue. But you went out and burned 378 files, according to your own admission. And every one of you, I think, said that you did it in order to hinder the operation of the draft. I am not questioning the morality of what you did. But people who violate the law in order to make a point must expect to be punished.

THOMAS MELVILLE. Your Honor, we are not arguing from a purely legal standpoint.

JOHN HOGAN. My question, Your Honor, concerns conscience. Did you tell the jury they could not act according to their conscience?

JUDGE. I said this to the defense: if you attempt to argue that the jury has the power to decide this case on the basis of conscience, the Court will interrupt and tell the jury of their duty.

JOHN HOGAN. But was the jury told they could not use their conscience in determining the truth—

JUDGE. I certainly did not tell them they could disregard their oath and let you off on sympathy, or because they thought you were sincere people. (DANIEL BERRIGAN *starts to interrupt as he crosses* C. MARY MOYLAN *and* MARJORIE MELVILLE *stand.*) I do not mind saying that this is the first time the question of conscience has been raised in this court.

DANIEL BERRIGAN. Your Honor, we are having great difficulty in trying to adjust to the atmosphere of a court from which the world is excluded, and the events that brought us here are excluded deliberately by the charge to the jury.

JUDGE. They were not excluded. The question—

DANIEL BERRIGAN. May I continue?

JUDGE. Well, you say they were excluded.

DANIEL BERRIGAN. (*Crosses up to* JUDGE, *then toward jury box.*) They were. Our moral passion was excluded. It is as though we were subjects of an autopsy, were being dismembered by people who wondered whether or not we had a soul. We are sure that we have a soul. It is our soul that brought us here. It is our soul that got us in trouble. It is our conception of man. But our moral passion is banished from this court. It is as though the legal process were an autopsy.

JUDGE. Well, I cannot match your poetic language. You made your points on the stand very persuasively, Father Berrigan. I admire you as a poet. But I think you simply do not understand the function of a court.

DANIEL BERRIGAN. I am sure that is true, Your Honor.

JUDGE. You admitted that you went to Catonsville with a purpose which requires your conviction. You wrote your purpose down in advance. Now I happen to have a job in which I am bound by an oath of office. Not only by an oath of office but by a long tradition of law, of which we are very proud in this country. We are proud of the Constitution of the United States. We are proud of the rights that people have under it. If you had done this thing in many countries of the world, you would not be standing here. You would have been in your coffins long ago. (DARST *crosses to* DEFENSE. DEFENDANTS *fan out across stage.*) Now, nobody is going to draw and quarter you. You may be convicted by the jury; and if you are, I certainly propose to give you every opportunity to say what you want.

DANIEL BERRIGAN. Your Honor, you speak very movingly of your understanding of what it is to be a judge. I wish to ask whether or not reverence for the law does not also require a judge to interpret and adjust the law to the needs of the people here and now. I believe that no tradition can remain a mere dead inheritance. It is a living inheritance which we must continue to offer to the living. Isn't it possible then to include in the law certain important questions of conscience, to include them nonetheless, and thereby to bring the tradition to life again for the sake of the people?

JUDGE. Well, I think there are two answers to that. You speak to me as a man and as a judge. As a man, I would be a very funny sort if I were not moved by your sincerity on the stand . . . and by your views. I agree with you completely, as a person. We can never accomplish what we would like to accomplish, or give a better life to people, if we are going to keep on spending so much money for war. But it is very unfortunate, the issue of the war cannot be presented as sharply as you would like. The basic principle of our law is that we do things in an orderly fashion. People cannot take the law into their own hands.

DAVID DARST. (*Crossing to* JUDGE.) Your Honor, does that include the President of the United States?

JUDGE. Of course, the President must obey the law.

THOMAS LEWIS. He hasn't.

JUDGE. Well, if the President has not obeyed the law, there is very little that can be done. . . .

GEORGE MISCHE. (*Crossing* D.) And that is one of the things this trial is all about.

JUDGE. . . . except not to reelect him.

(DEFENDANTS *shift positions.*)

DANIEL BERRIGAN. Your Honor, you have referred to the war question as one which may be either political or legal. Suppose it were considered as a question of life and death. Could that be appropriately raised here?

JUDGE. Well, again, that is poetic speech. I am not sure what the legal proposition is. I understand why it seems a matter of life and death to you. Of course, the war is a matter of life and death to all the boys who fight in it. It is a matter of life and death to people in Vietnam.

MARY MOYLAN. Your Honor, I think you said previously that you had a great deal of respect for the law and the Constitution of the United States. I would like to call that respect into question, if you are unwilling to do anything about a war which is a violation of our legal tradition and the United States Constitution.

JUDGE. Well, I understand your point, but I cannot appoint you either my legal or my spiritual advisor, my dear.

GEORGE MISCHE. (*Crossing up to* JUDGE.) We have people from the peace movement here. Will you allow them to file a brief in your court, calling into question the entire Vietnam war; and will you be willing to review the charge in its entirety? Whatever decision you make can then be submitted to the Supreme Court.

JUDGE. But you have to have a case—

GEORGE MISCHE. You have to break the law first—

JUDGE. —that can be brought into court.

GEORGE MISCHE. —you have to break a law. It seems that, before we can get a judge to face the situation, you have to break a law, as Martin Luther King found out.

JUDGE. If you had gotten legal advice, I am sure you would have been advised that there are better ways to raise this question than the way you raised it at Catonsville.

THOMAS LEWIS. Your Honor, one question: I have been called an honest and a just man in this courtroom. I appreciate that. But the reality is that I leave this room in chains. I am taken back to prison. How do you explain this?

JUDGE. Good character is not a defense for breaking the law. That is the only way I can explain it.

PHILIP BERRIGAN. (*Crosses* c.) Your Honor, I think we would be less than honest with you if we did not restate our attitude. Simply, we have lost confidence in the institutions of the country, including the courts and our own churches. I think this has been a rational process on our part. We have come to our conclusion slowly and painfully. We have lost confidence, because we do not believe any longer that these institutions are reformable. They are unable to provide the type of change that justice calls for. This has occurred because the law is no longer serving the needs of the people; which is a pretty good definition of morality.

JUDGE. I can understand how you feel. I think the only difference between us is that I believe the institutions can do what you believe they cannot do.

PHILIP BERRIGAN. Our question remains: how much time is left this country, this magnificent, frantic, insane, nation-empire to which God has entrusted so much of the future of mankind? That is the question we are concerned about: man's survival.

JUDGE. I assure you I am concerned about your question selfishly, for my grandchildren, as well as for everybody else. It is a serious thing.

GEORGE MISCHE. Change could come if one judge would rule on the war. If one judge would act, the war could not continue as it does.

JUDGE. I think you misunderstand the organization of

the United States. One judge ruling on it would not end the war. Each judge must do his best with what comes before him.

DANIEL BERRIGAN. (*Crosses* D. C. *Interrupting.*) We want to thank you, Your Honor; I speak for the others. But we do not want the edge taken off what we have tried to say by any implication that we are seeking mercy in this court. We welcome the rigors of this court. Our intention in appearing here after Catonsville was to be useful to the poor of the world, to the black people of the world and of our own country, and to those in our prisons who have no voice. We do not wish that primary blade of intention to be honed down to no edge at all by a gentlemen's agreement, whereby you agree with us and we with you. We do not agree with you, and we thank you.

JUDGE. All right.

DANIEL BERRIGAN. (*Reacting to suggestion from* MARJORIE MELVILLE.) Could we finish with a prayer? Would that be against your wishes? We would like to recite the "Our Father" with our friends.

JUDGE. I will be glad to hear from the government's counsel as to his advice.

PROSECUTION. The government has no objection and, in fact, rather welcomes the idea.

(DEFENDANTS *form a semicircle, clasp hands and recite the "Our Father."*)

DEFENDANTS. Our Father, who art in heaven, Hallowed be thy name. Thy kingdom come, thy will be done on earth as it is in heaven. Give us this day our daily bread, and forgive us our trespasses as we forgive those who trespass against us. And lead us not into temptation, but deliver us from evil, for thine is the kingdom and the power and the glory forever. Amen.

TAPE. (CLERK.) The taking of the verdict in Criminal Action No. 28111, the United States of America against Philip Berrigan, Daniel Berrigan, Thomas Lewis, David

Darst, John Hogan, Marjorie Melville, Thomas Melville, George Mische and Mary Moylan. Members of the jury, what say you: is the defendant John Hogan guilty of the matters whereof he stands indicted?

(*As each* DEFENDANT's *name is called, he crosses* D. *to form a tight group.*)

TAPE. (FOREMAN.) We find John Hogan guilty.

TAPE. (CLERK.) Members of the jury, what say you: Is the defendant Marjorie Melville guilty?

TAPE. (FOREMAN.) We find Marjorie Melville guilty.

TAPE. (CLERK.) Members of the jury, what say you: Is the defendant Thomas Melville guilty?

TAPE. (FOREMAN.) We find Thomas Melville guilty. We find David Darst guilty. We find Mary Moylan guilty. We find Philip Berrigan guilty. We find Daniel Berrigan guilty. We find Thomas Lewis guilty. We find George Mische guilty.

JUDGE. Now, is there anything further that the government or the defendants wish brought to the attention of the Court?

DANIEL BERRIGAN. We would simply like to thank the Court and the prosecution. We agree that this is the greatest day of our lives.

CURTAIN

PROPERTY PLOT

PRESET:

Onstage:
Lectern with altar cloth D. C.
Microphone (practical) in judge's box
Bible on D. L. corner of judge's box
Swivel chair in judge's box
2 swivel chairs at desk positions

Off Right:
Flag
R. witness rail
Wooden draft file boxes with charred files

Off Left:
2 trash burners (wired together)
2 witness rails (stacked L. rail on top)

Personal:

JUDGE:
Gavel
Legal pad
Glasses

DARST:
Glasses

PROSECUTION:
Gray attaché case (containing file folders, legal pads, photos, notes)

DEFENSE:
Black briefcase (containing same as above)

DAN:
Black notebook with meditation and pencil

51

COSTUME PLOT

DANIEL BERRIGAN:
Black coat, black pants, black turtleneck sweater, black socks, black shoes (personal), medallion and chain, 2 white T-shirts.

PHILIP BERRIGAN:
Black coat, black pants, black belt, clerical vest, 2 clerical collars, black shoes (personal), black socks, 2 white T-shirts.

THOMAS LEWIS:
Green suit, white shirt, brown tie, brown belt, brown shoes (personal), black socks.

DAVID DARST:
Black coat, black pants, glasses, black clerical vest, white shirt, black shoes, black socks.

JOHN HOGAN:
Brown suit, brown belt, white shirt, black and brown figured tie, brown shoes, black socks.

THOMAS MELVILLE:
Brown suit, brown belt, white shirt, green tie, brown shoes (personal), black socks.

GEORGE MISCHE:
Maroon plaid sports coat, brown pants, black socks, 2 gold velour sweaters, brown belt, brown suede desert boots.

JUDGE:
Brown glen plaid suit (personal), brown shoes (personal), socks (personal), white shirt (personal), tie (personal), robe, glasses, mustache.

DEFENSE:
Blue suit, white shirt, blue and red tie, gold tie clip (personal), brown shoes (personal), black socks, brown belt.

PROSECUTION:
Gray suit with vest, white shirt, black shoes, glasses (personal), black socks, blue and gold striped tie, black belt.

MARJORIE MELVILLE:
Navy and white dress, wrist watch, brown loafers, 2 pairs pantyhose.

MARY MOYLAN:
Green crepe dress, orange and brown paisley scarf, bell on leather thong, brown purse, 2 pairs pantyhose, brown pumps.

WITNESS:
Brown and white suit, brown velvet hat, 2 pairs pantyhose, brown pumps, brown purse, blue and lavender print blouse, brown gloves.

3 MARSHALS:
Navy police uniforms, black shoes, blue shirt, black tie, black belt.

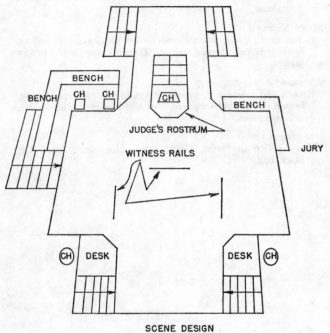

SCENE DESIGN
"THE TRIAL OF THE CATONSVILLE NINE"

Other Publications for Your Interest

A LESSON FROM ALOES
(LITTLE THEATRE—DRAMA)
By ATHOL FUGARD

2 men, 1 woman—Interior

N.Y. Drama Critics Circle Award, Best Play of the Year. Set in a house in a white district of Port Elizabeth, South Africa, in 1963 this important new work by a truly major dramatist gives a compelling portrait of a society caught in the grip of a police state, and the effect it has on individuals. We are in the house of a liberal Afrikaner and his wife. He has been actively involved in anti-apartheid activity; she is recovering from a recent nervous breakdown brought about by a police raid on their home. They are waiting for a Black family to come to dinner (in South Africa, this is an absolutely forbidden act of insurrection). The Black family never arrives; but the head of the family does. He has just been released from prison and plans to flee South Africa—after first confronting the Afrikaner with the charge that he has betrayed him. "Exile, madness, utter loneliness—these are the only alternatives Mr. Fugard's characters have. What makes 'Aloes' so moving is the playwright's insistence on the heroism and integrity of these harsh choices."—N.Y. Times. "Immensely moving."—N.Y. Post. "One of the few dramatists in the world whose work really matters."—Newsweek.   (#14146)

(Royalty, $60–$40, where available.)

MEETINGS
(BLACK GROUPS—COMEDY)
By MUSTAPHA MATURA

1 man, 2 women—Interiors

Greatly-acclaimed in its recent Off-Broadway production at New York's excellent Phoenix Theatre, *Meetings* is set in an ultra-modern kitchen which would be the dream of any American family—but it is in fast-developing Trinidad and is well-stocked with everything but food, much to the consternation of the husband, a successful engineer. His wife, an equally successful marketing executive, spends too much time at "meetings" (so does he)—and neither has time to actually *use* their kitchen. While the husband pines for some good down-home cooking, the wife is off pushing a new brand of cigarette ("Trini" is being used as a test-market). Soon, the local people are coughing up blood, and many die—apparently from the effects of smoking the new cigarette. Eventually, the husband goes "back to nature" and the wife succumbs to her own product. "An amazing piece of theatre . . . a highly literal parable about the poisoning of the tropical isle by modern commercialism."—Women's Wear Daily. "A bright, sharp comedy that turns into a sombre fable before our eyes."—The New Yorker.   (#15659)

(Royalty, $50–$35.)

Other Publications for Your Interest

COMING ATTRACTIONS
(ADVANCED GROUPS—COMEDY WITH MUSIC)

By TED TALLY, music by JACK FELDMAN, lyrics by BRUCE SUSSMAN and FELDMAN

5 men, 2 women—Unit Set

Lonnie Wayne Burke has the requisite viciousness to be a media celebrity—but he lacks vision. When we meet him, he is holding only four people hostage in a laundromat. There aren't any cops much less reporters around, because they're across town where some guy is holding *50* hostages. But, a talent agent named Manny sees possibilities in Lonnie Wayne. He devises a criminal persona for him by dressing him in a skeleton costume and sending him door-to-door, murdering people as "The Hallowe'en Killer". He is captured, and becomes an instant celebrity, performing on TV shows. When his fame starts to wane, he crashes the Miss America Pageant disguised as Miss Wyoming to kill Miss America on camera. However, he falls in love with her, and this eventually leads to his downfall. Lonnie ends up in the electric chair, and is fried "live" on prime-time TV as part of a jazzy production number! "Fizzles with pixilated laughter."—Time. "I don't often burst into gales of laughter in the theatre; here, I found myself rocking with guffaws."—New York Mag. "Vastly entertaining."—Newark Star-Ledger.

(Royalty, $50–$40.)

SORROWS OF STEPHEN
(ADVANCED GROUPS—COMEDY)

By PETER PARNELL

4 men, 5 women—Unit set

Stephen Hurt is a headstrong, impetuous young man—an irrepressible romantic—he's unable not to be in love. One of his models is Goethe's tragic hero, Werther, but as a contemporary New Yorker, he's adaptable. The end of an apparently undying love is followed by the birth of a grand new passion. And as he believes there's a literary precedent for all romantic possibilities justifying his choices—so with enthusiasm bordering on fickleness, he turns from Tolstoy, to Stendhal or Balzac. And Stephen's never discouraged—he can withstand rivers of rejection. (From the N.Y. Times.) And so his affairs—real and tentative—begin when his girl friend leaves him. He makes a romantic stab at a female cab driver, passes an assignation note to an unknown lady at the opera, flirts with an accessible waitress—and then has a tragic-with-comic-overtones, wild affair with his best friend's fiancée. "Breezy and buoyant. A real romantic comedy, sophisticated and sentimental, with an ageless attitude toward the power of positive love."—N.Y. Times.

(Slightly Restricted. Royalty, $50–$40, where available)

Other Publications for Your Interest

TALKING WITH . . .
(LITTLE THEATRE)
By JANE MARTIN

11 women—Bare stage

Here, at last, is the collection of eleven extraordinary monologues for eleven actresses which had them on their feet cheering at the famed Actors Theatre of Louisville—audiences, critics and, yes, even jaded theatre professionals. The mysteriously pseudonymous Jane Martin is truly a "find", a new writer with a wonderfully idiosyncratic style, whose characters alternately amuse, move and frighten us always, however, speaking to use from the depths of their souls. The characters include a baton twirler who has found God through twirling; a fundamentalist snake handler, an ex-rodeo rider crowded out of the life she has cherished by men in 3-piece suits who want her to dress up "like Minnie damn Mouse in a tutu"; an actress willing to go to any length to get a job; and an old woman who claims she once saw a man with "cerebral walrus" walk into a McDonald's and be healed by a Big Mac. "Eleven female monologues, of which half a dozen verge on brilliance."—London Guardian. "Whoever (Jane Martin) is, she's a writer with an original imagination."—Village Voice. "With Jane Martin, the monologue has taken on a new poetic form, intensive in its method and revelatory in its impact."—Philadelphia Inquirer. "A dramatist with an original voice . . . (these are) tales about enthusiasms that become obsessions, eccentric confessionals that levitate with religious symbolism and gladsome humor."—N.Y. Times. *Talking With . . .* is the 1982 winner of the American Theatre Critics Association Award for Best Regional Play.　(#22009)

(Royalty, $60–$40.
If individual monologues are done separately: Royalty, $15–$10.)

HAROLD AND MAUDE
(ADVANCED GROUPS—COMEDY)
By COLIN HIGGINS

9 men, 8 women—Various settings

Yes: *the Harold and Maude!* This is a stage adaptation of the wonderful movie about the suicidal 19 year-old boy who finally learns how to truly *live* when he meets up with that delightfully whacky octogenarian, Maude. Harold is the proverbial Poor Little Rich Kid. His alienation has caused him to attempt suicide several times, though these attempts are more cries for attention than actual attempts. His peculiar attachment to Maude, whom he meets at a funeral (a mutual passion), is what saves him—and what captivates us. This new stage version, a hit in France directed by the internationally-renowned Jean-Louis Barrault, will certainly delight both afficionados of the film and new-comers to the story. "Offbeat upbeat comedy."—Christian Science Monitor.　(#10032)

(Royalty, $60–$40.)

A Man for All Seasons
By ROBERT BOLT

DRAMA—2 ACTS—11 men, 3 women—Unit set

Garlands of awards and critical praise greeted this long-run success in both New York and London. In both productions Paul Scofield was pronounced brilliant for his portrayal of Sir Thomas More in his last years as Lord Chancellor of England during the reign of Henry VIII. When Henry failed to obtain from the Pope a divorce from Catherine of Aragon, in order to marry Anne Boleyn, he rebelled by requiring his subjects to sign an Act of Supremacy making him both spiritual and temporal leader of England. More could not in conscience comply. Neither Thomas Cromwell, nor Cardinal Wolsey nor the King himself could get a commitment from him. He resisted anything heroic; he wanted only to maintain his integrity and belief in silence. But this was treason, and his very silence led him to his death. " '*A Man For All Seasons*' is the ageless and inspiring echo of the small voice that calls to us: 'To thine own self be true.' . . . A smashing hit . . . A titantic hit . . . In conception and execution it is a masterpiece."—*N. Y. Journal-American*.

(Royalty, $50-$25.)

J. B.
By ARCHIBALD MacLEISH

VERSE DRAMA—2 ACTS

12 men, 9 women—Interior

Winner of the Pulitzer Prize for playwriting

The following is from the review of *J. B.* by Brooks Atkinson in the *New York Times:* "Looking around at the wreckage and misery of the modern world, Mr. MacLeish has written a fresh and exalting morality that has great stature. In an inspired performance yesterday evening, it seemed to me one of the memorable works of the century as verse, as drama and as spiritual inquiry. The stage is set . . . in the form of a circus tent . . . Two circus peddlers make whimsical use of the tent by playing God and the Devil. Presently we are deep in the unanswered problems of man's relationship to God in an era of cruel injustices. J. B., a modern business man rich with blessings, is Mr. MacLeish's counterpart of the immortal Job . . . J. B. is brought down by the terrible affliction of our century—deaths and violent catastrophes that seem to have no cause or meaning . . . The glory of Mr. MacLeish's play is that, as in the Book of Job, J. B does not curse God. When he is reunited with his wife, two humbled but valiant people accept the universe, agree to begin life over again, expecting no justice but unswerving in their devotion to God.

(Royalty, $50-$25.)

Other Publications for Your Interest

THE DRESSER
(LITTLE THEATRE—DRAMA)
By RONALD HARWOOD

10 men, 3 women—Complete interior

Sir, the last of the great, but dying, breed of English actor/managers, is in a very bad way tonight. As his dresser tries valiantly to prepare him to go on stage as King Lear, Sir is having great difficulty remembering who and where he is, let alone Lear's lines. With a Herculean effort on the part of Norman, the dresser, Sir finally does make it on stage, and through the performance—no thanks to the bombs of the *Luftwaffe*, which are falling all around the theatre (the play takes place back stage on an English provincial theatre during an air raid during World War II). It is to be Sir's last performance, though; for backstage in his dressing room after the performance, the worn out old trouper dies—leaving his company—and, in particular, his loyal dresser—alone with their loneliness. "A stirring evening . . . burns with a love of the theater that conquers all . . . perfectly observed, devilishly entertaining backstage lore."—N.Y. Times. "Sheer wonderful theatricality . . . I think you'll love it as much as I did."— N.Y. Daily News. "Enthralling, funny and touching. Lovingly delineated dramatic portraits . . . Almost any actor would jump at them."—N.Y. Post. "A wonderfully affectionate and intelligent play about the theatre."—The Guardian, London.

(For Future Release. Royalty, $60–$40, when available.)

EQUUS
(LITTLE THEATRE—MORALITY)
By PETER SHAFFER

5 men, 4 women, 6 actors to play horses—Basic setting

Martin Dysart, a psychiatrist, is confronted with Alan Strang, a boy who has blinded six horses. To the owner of the horses the horror is simple: he was unlucky enough to employ 'a loony'. To the boy's parents it is a hideous mystery: Alan had always adored horses, and although Dora Strang may have been a slightly overindulgent mother and Frank Strang a slightly tetchy father, they both loved their son. To Dysart it is a psychological puzzle to be untangled and pain to be alleviated . . . or rather, given his profession, that is what it ought to be. As it turns out, it is something far more complex and disturbing: a confrontation with himself as well as with Alan, in which he comes to an inescapable view of man's need to worship and the distortions forced on that need by "civilized" society. Since this is a story of discovery, the reader's excitement would be diminished by a detailed account of its development. "The closest I have seen a contemporary play come to reanimating the spirit of mystery that makes the stage a place of breathless discovery rather than a classroom for rational demonstration. Mr. Shaffer may have been trying for just such iconography—a portrait of the drives that lead men to crucify themselves—there. Here I think he's found it."—Walter Kerr, N.Y. Times.

(Royalty, $50–$35.)

THE SEA HORSE
EDWARD J. MOORE

(Little Theatre) Drama
1 Man, 1 Woman, Interior

It is a play that is, by turns, tender, ribald, funny and suspenseful. Audiences everywhere will take it to their hearts because it is touched with humanity and illuminates with glowing sympathy the complexities of a man-woman relationship. Set in a West Coast waterfront bar, the play is about Harry Bales, a seaman, who, when on shore leave, usually heads for "The Sea Horse," the bar run by Gertrude Blum, the heavy, unsentimental proprietor. Their relationship is purely physical and, as the play begins, they have never confided their private yearnings to each other. But this time Harry has returned with a dream: to buy a charter fishing boat and to have a son by Gertrude. She, in her turn, has made her life one of hard work, by day, and nocturnal love-making; she has encased her heart behind a facade of toughness, utterly devoid of sentimentality, because of a failed marriage. Irwin's play consists in the ritual of "dance" courtship by Harry of Gertrude, as these two outwardly abrasive characters fight, make up, fight again, spin dreams, deflate them, make love and reveal their long locked-up secrets.

"A burst of brilliance!"—*N.Y. Post.* "I was touched close to tears!"—*Village Voice.* "A must! An incredible love story. A beautiful play!"—*Newhouse Newspapers.* "A major new playwright!"—*Variety.*

ROYALTY, $50-$35

THE AU PAIR MAN
HUGH LEONARD

(Little Theatre) Comedy
1 Man, 1 Woman, Interior

The play concerns a rough Irish bill collector named Hartigan, who becomes a love slave and companion to an English lady named Elizabeth, who lives in a cluttered London town house, which looks more like a museum for a British Empire on which the sun has long set. Even the door bell chimes out the national anthem. Hartigan is immediately conscripted into her service in return for which she agrees to teach him how to be a gentleman rather after the fashion of a reverse Pygmalion. The play is a wild one, and is really the neverending battle between England and Ireland. Produced to critical acclaim at Lincoln Center's Vivian Beaumont Theatre.

ROYALTY, $50-$35

Other Publications for Your Interest

SEA MARKS
(LITTLE THEATRE—DRAMA)
By GARDNER McKAY

1 woman, 1 man—Unit set

Winner of L.A. Drama Critics Circle Award "Best Play." This is the "funny, touching, bittersweet tale" (Sharbutt, A.P.) of a fisherman living on a remote island to the west of Ireland who has fallen in love with, in retrospect, a woman he's glimpsed only once. Unschooled in letter-writing, he tries his utmost to court by mail and, after a year-and-a-half, succeeds in arranging a rendezvous at which, to his surprise, she persuades him to live with her in Liverpool. Their love affair ends only when he is forced to return to the life he better understands. "A masterpiece." (The Tribune, Worcester, Mass.) "Utterly winning," (John Simon, New York Magazine.) "There's abundant humor, surprisingly honest humor, that grows between two impossible partners. The reaching out and the fearful withdrawal of two people who love each other but whose lives simply cannot be fused: a stubborn, decent, attractive and touching collision of temperments, honest in portraiture and direct in speech. High marks for SEA MARKS!" (Walter Kerr, New York Times.) "Fresh as a May morning. A lovely, tender and happily humorous love story." (Elliot Norton, Boston Herald American.) "It could easily last forever in actors' classrooms and audition studios." (Oliver, The New Yorker)

(Slightly Restricted. Royalty, $50–$35)

THE WOOLGATHERER
(LITTLE THEATRE—DRAMA)
By WILLIAM MASTROSIMONE

1 man, 1 woman—Interior

In a dreary Philadelphia apartment lives Rose, a shy and slightly creepy five-and-dime salesgirl. Into her life saunters Cliff, a hard-working, hard-drinking truck driver—who has picked up Rose and been invited back to her room. Rose is an innocent whose whole life centers around reveries and daydreams. He is rough and witty—but it's soon apparent—just as starved for love as she is. This little gem of a play was a recent success at New York's famed Circle Repertory starring Peter Weller and Patricia Wettig. Actors take note: *The Woolgatherer* has several excellent monologues. ". . . energy, compassion and theatrical sense are there."—N.Y. Times. ". . . another emotionally wrenching experience no theatre enthusiast should miss."—Rex Reed. "Mastrosimone writes consistently witty and sometimes lyrical dialogue."—New York Magazine. "(Mastrosimone) has a knack for composing wildly humorous lines at the same time that he is able to penetrate people's hearts and dreams."—Hollywood Reporter.

(Slightly Restricted. Royalty, $50–$35, where available.)

Other Publications for Your Interest

THE CAINE MUTINY COURT-MARTIAL
(ALL GROUPS—DRAMA)

By HERMAN WOUK

19 men (6 nonspeaking)—Curtained set, desks, chairs and
dark blue uniforms of the U.S. Navy.

"The Caine Mutiny," the Pulitzer Prize novel hailed by critics as "the best sea story" and "the best World War II novel," has been adapted by the author in a version which is superior to the novel "in the artfullness of its craftsmanship." (N.Y. Herald Tribune.) "Enormously exciting. It is the modern stage at its best," said the Daily News. "Magnificent theatre," said the Mirror and the Journal-American. It is the court-martial proceedings against a young upright lieutenant who relieved his captain of command in the midst of a harrowing typhoon on the grounds that the captain was psychopathic in the crisis, and was directing the ship and its crew to its destruction. The odds and naval tradition are against the lieutenant. But as the witnesses and experts, some serious, some unwittingly comic, cross the scene of the trial, the weakness in the character of the captain is slowly revealed in a devastating picture of disintegration. An ideal play for all groups.

(Royalty, $50-$25.)

MEDAL OF HONOR RAG
(LITTLE THEATRE—DRAMA)

By TOM COLE

3 men (2 white, 1 black)

In an army hospital two very dissimilar men confront one another in a verbal sparring match. One, a psychiatrist—the other, "D.J.", a black ex-serviceman and holder of the Congressional Medal of Honor; an "honor" of that hangs on him like an ironic albatross. They also share one common experience—and guilt—they are both survivors in which many others perished. The psychiatrist gradually draws out of D.J. all the guilt, horror and disgust which left him traumatized. Always on guard against "whitie" and his values, D.J. is gradually revealed as a sensitive, intelligent, man nearly destroyed by his Viet Nam experience. His barriers crumbling, D.J. turns on the psychiatrist, exposing the man behind the professional facade. Yet D.J. desperately hopes—and the psychiatrist believes—he can be helped. But before another interview takes place, D.J. goes AWOL—and to get money for unpaid bills—is killed in an attempted robbery. "Cole has handled explosive with great intelligence and rich human understanding . . . beautifully written . . ."—WWD.

(Royalty, $50-$35.)

Other Publications for Your Interest

PAST TENSE
(LITTLE THEATRE—DRAMA)
By JACK ZEMAN

1 man, 1 woman, 2 optional men—Interior

This compelling new play is about the breakup of a marriage. It is set on the day Emily and Ralphy Michaelson, a prosperous middle-aged couple, break off a union of 27 years. As they confront each other in their packed-up living room one final time, they alternately taunt and caress one another. She has never forgiven him for a petty infidelity of years ago. He has never forgiven her for her inability to express grief over the long-ago accidental death of their youngest child. In a series of flashbacks, Mr. Zeman dredges up the pivotal events of his characters' lives. Barbara Feldon and Laurence Luckinbill starred on Broadway in this at times humorous, and ultimately very moving play by a talented new playwright. ''. . . rich in theatrical devices, sassy talk and promising themes.''—N.Y. Times. ''There is no doubt that Zeman can write. His backbiting, backlashing dialogue has considerable gusto—it belts out with a most impressively muscular vigor and intellectual vivacity.''—N.Y. Post.

(Royalty, $50–$35)

SCENES AND REVELATIONS
(ALL GROUPS—DRAMA)
By ELAN GARONZIK

3 men, 4 women—Platform set

Set in 1894 at the height of America's westward movement, the play portrays the lives of four Pennsylvania sisters who decide not to move west, but to England. It opens with the sisters prepared to leave their farm and birthplace forever. Then a series of lyrical flashbacks dramatize the tender and frustrating romances of the women. Rebecca, the youngest, marries and moves west to Nebraska, only to find she is ill-prepared for pioneer life. Millie, a bohemian artist, falls in love with the farm boy next door; when he marries a woman without Millie's worldly aspirations, she is crushed. Charlotte, a nurse, is rejected by her doctor on religious principles. Only Helena, the eldest, has the promise of a bright and bold life in California with Samuel, the farm's manager. However, Rebecca's tragic return east moves the sisters to unite for the promise of a better life in England. ''A deeply human play . . . a rocket to the moon of imagination,'' Claudia Cassidy—WFMT, Chicago. ''Humanly full . . . glimmers with revelation,'' Elliott—Chicago Sun-Times. ''The play is a beauty,'' Sharp—WWD. ''A deep understanding of women and their relationships with men,'' Barnes—New York Post.

(Royalty, $50–$35.)